OFFICIALLY
WITHDRAWN

TOOLS FOR CAREGIVERS

- **ATOS:** 0.4
- **GRL:** C
- **WORD COUNT:** 43

- **CURRICULUM CONNECTIONS:** animals, insects, nature

Skills to Teach

- **HIGH-FREQUENCY WORDS:** a, are, I, in, see, they
- **CONTENT WORDS:** ants, climb, drink, eat, lift, line, small, together, walk, work
- **PUNCTUATION:** periods
- **WORD STUDY:** long /e/, spelled ea (eat); long /e/, spelled ee (see); multisyllable word (together)
- **TEXT TYPE:** information report

Before Reading Activities

- Read the title and give a simple statement of the main idea.
- Have students "walk" though the book and talk about what they see in the pictures.
- Introduce new vocabulary by having students predict the first letter and locate the word in the text.
- Discuss any unfamiliar concepts that are in the text.

After Reading Activities

Explain to readers that a group of ants is called a colony. Members of the colony work together. What did the readers notice ants do together from reading the book? Can they name any other kinds of insects or animals that live together in a group? What are the insect or animal groups called? List their examples on the board.

Tadpole Books are published by Jump!, 5357 Penn Avenue South, Minneapolis, MN 55419, www.jumplibrary.com

Copyright ©2019 Jump!. International copyright reserved in all countries. No part of this book may be reproduced in any form without written permission from the publisher.

Editor: Jenna Trnka **Designer:** Michelle Sonnek

Photo Credits: NaturePL/SuperStock, cover; Antagain/iStock, 1, 4–5, 16bm; Tom Wang/Shutterstock, 2–3 (boy); Vlad Siaber/Shutterstock, 2–3 (log); Mirek Kijewski/Shutterstock, 2–3 (ants); Robert Blouin/Shutterstock, 6–7, 16tr; Maleo/Shutterstock, 8–9, 16tm; Ivan Kuzmin/Shutterstock, 10–11, 16bl; Andrey Pavlov/Shutterstock, 12–13, 16tl; frank60/Shutterstock, 14–15, 16br.

Library of Congress Cataloging-in-Publication Data
Names: Nilsen, Genevieve, author.
Title: I see ants / by Genevieve Nilsen.
Description: Minneapolis, MN: Jump!, Inc., (2019) | Series: Backyard bugs | Includes index.
Identifiers: LCCN 2018016029 (print) | LCCN 2018017335 (ebook) | ISBN 9781641282185 (ebook) | ISBN 9781641282161 (hardcover: alk. paper) | ISBN 9781641282178 (paperback)
Subjects: LCSH: Ants—Juvenile literature.
Classification: LCC QL568.F7 (ebook) | LCC QL568.F7 N53 2018 (print) | DDC 595.79/6—dc23
LC record available at https://lccn.loc.gov/2018016029

BACKYARD BUGS

I SEE ANTS

by Genevieve Nilsen

TABLE OF CONTENTS

tadpole
books

I SEE ANTS

I see ants.

They are small.

I see ants.

They walk in a line.

I see ants.

6

apple

They eat.

I see ants.

water

They drink.

I see ants.

They lift.

I see ants.

They climb.

I see ants.

14

They work together.

WORDS TO KNOW

climb

drink

eat

lift

walk

work

INDEX